Math Fun with Puppies and Kittens

Learning How to
MEASURE

with Puppies and Kittens

Enslow Publishing
101 W. 23rd Street
Suite 240
New York, NY 10011
USA

enslow.com

Eustacia Moldovo
and Patricia J. Murphy

Words to Know

centimeter A unit of measurement. A meter has 100 centimeters.

height The measurement from the bottom to the top of something.

inch A unit of measurement. A foot has 12 inches. A yard has 36 inches.

length The distance from one end of an object to another.

measure To figure out the size, weight, or amount of an object.

measurements The height, length, width, weight, or amount of something.

nonstandard Not the usual units of measurements used by most people.

standard The usual units of measurements used by most people.

width The distance from one side of an object to the other side.

Contents

Measurements

When you **measure** something, you find the size of it. Units that tell you the **length**, **height**, **width**, weight, or amount of something are called **measurements**. You can tell how big or small something is by its measurements.

BIG!

small!

Measurements are important. You use them to know how tall people are, how far away places are, how big or small to make clothing, and much more!

In this book, you will measure cute puppies and kittens to learn about measurements!

Learn Nonstandard Measurements

You can use **nonstandard** or **standard** measurements to find the size of something. Examples of nonstandard measurements are the number of things like paper clips, cubes, erasers, hands, fingers, or shoes that are the same size as the object.

Measure this kitten in erasers, cubes, and shoes.

The kitten is **6** erasers tall.

The kitten is **3** cubes tall.   The kitten is **2** shoes tall.

Using all these different objects makes the kitten's height all different numbers. Erasers, cubes, and shoes are different sizes. And your shoes may be a different size from your friend's shoes. Even if both of you used your shoes to measure the kitten, each of you would still get a different number. This can be confusing.

How can you and your friend get the same measurements for the kitten? Use standard measurements. Find out what those are on the next page.

Learn Standard Measurements

Standard measurements have the same size units no matter who uses them. In the United States, people use the inch, foot, and yard to measure height, length, and width. In most other countries, people use centimeters and meters. This is known as the metric system.

The most common measuring tools are the ruler, yardstick, tape measure, and meter stick. Rulers and tape measures have both inches and centimeters on them.

tape measure

ruler

yardstick

meter stick

A ruler is **one foot** long. A foot is **12 inches**.

A yardstick is **one yard** long. A yard is **36 inches**, or **3 feet**.

A tape measure is used when something is too big to measure with a ruler or yardstick. Tape measures come in different lengths.

A meter stick is one meter, or **100 centimeters,** long.

Measure this kitten using three different measuring tools.

The ruler says she is **6** inches tall.

The yardstick says she is **6** inches tall, too.

The tape measure also says she is **6** inches tall.

All of these tools use the inch as the unit of measurement. That's why you get the same answer for all three!

Learn How to Measure

There are three steps to follow when measuring:

1. Place your measuring tool next to the thing you are measuring. Let's practice with a puppy and a yardstick!

2. Line up the end of the yardstick that starts with **0** with one end of the puppy.

3. Look at the other end of the yardstick. The number at the other end of the puppy is the measurement.

This puppy is **16** inches long from nose to tail!

Learn to Measure Height

Different things are different heights. Height is the measurement from the bottom to the top of something, or how tall or high it is. Puppies and kittens come in many different sizes. Measure the heights of these two puppies in inches and centimeters.

Why 100?

Centi comes from the Latin word centum, which means "hundred." This is why 100 centimeters equals one meter. This is also where we get "century" (100 years) and "cent" (100 cents equals one American dollar).

Charlie the Chihuahua is **5** inches tall or almost **13** centimeters tall.

Dana the Great Dane is **11** inches tall or **28** centimeters tall.

A centimeter is smaller than an inch.

Measure the Height of the Scratching Post

Kittens need scratching posts high enough to stretch their bodies. Measure Piper's scratching post.

The height of the scratching post is **24** inches.

How tall is Piper when she stretches?

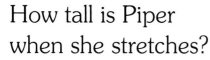

A Foot Is a Foot Long

Long ago, a foot was a little smaller than 12 inches. Today 12 inches is about the length of a man's foot.

Piper is **22** inches tall when she stretches.

The scratching post's height of **24** inches is more than **22** inches. It is tall enough for Piper to stretch against.

Measure the Heights of the Jumps

Many puppies enjoy catching Frisbees.

23 24 25 26 27
10 cm = 100

Benny

Callie

8 9 10 11 12
10 MILLIMETERS

How high did Benny jump to catch the Frisbee?

How high did Callie jump to catch the Frisbee?

Benny jumped **25** centimeters into the air.

Callie jumped **10** centimeters into the air.

Which puppy jumped higher? How much higher?

HINT: Use subtraction to find the answer.

See page 28 for the answers.

Number Lines for Subtracting

Number lines make subtracting easier. Start at the first number. Then move back the number of spaces equal to the second number. You will land on the answer.

0 1 2 3 4 5 6 7 8 9 10 11 12 13 14 **15** 16 17 18 19 20 21 22 23 24 **25**

Learn to Measure Length

Length is the distance from one end of an object to the other. Find out how long these ears are!

6

4

8

2

Buddy   Betty   Jill   Peanut

Buddy has ears that are **6** inches long.

Betty has ears that are **4** inches long.

Jill has ears that are **8** inches long.

Peanut has ears that are **2** inches long.

Who has the longest ears?

Who has the shortest ears?

How much longer are the longest ears than the shortest ears?

See page 28 for the answers.

Measure the Lengths of the Toys

Kittens are very playful. Many of them enjoy swatting at toys with feathers tied to the end of strings. Measure each of these cat toys.

Rudy's toy is **40** centimeters long.

Gizmo's toy is **20** centimeters long.

Darty's toy is **50** centimeters long.

The Earliest Yard

Long ago, a yard was the length of a man's belt.

Which cat toy is the longest?

Which cat toy is the shortest?

How much shorter is Gizmo's toy than Rudy's toy?

See page 28 for the answers.

21

Measure the Lengths of the Leashes

Many puppies like to go out on walks! But they should be on leashes to keep them safe. Measure how long these leashes are.

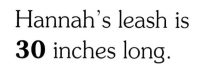

Hannah's leash is **30** inches long.

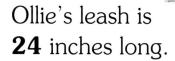

Ollie's leash is **24** inches long.

Leo's leash is **34** inches long.

Which leash is the longest?

Which leash is the shortest?

What is the difference between the two lengths?

See page 29 for the answers.

Learn to Measure Width

Width is the distance from one side of an object to the other side, or how wide it is. Measure the widths of these pet beds.

Sammy has a bed that is **22** inches wide.

Angel has a bed that is **16** inches wide.

Millie has a bed that is **13** inches wide.

Who has the biggest bed?

If the biggest bed was **2** inches wider, how wide would it be?

HINT: Use addition to find the answer.

See page 29 for the answers.

Number Lines for Adding

You can use number lines for adding, too. Start at the first number. Then move forward the number of spaces equal to the second number. You will land on the answer.

0 1 2 3 4 5 6 7 8 9 10 11 12 13 14 15 16 17 18 19 20 21 **22** 23 **24** 25

Measure the Widths of Their Bodies

Greta and Elvis have different body widths. Measure them.

The Earliest Inch

Long ago, an inch was the width of a man's thumb at the bottom of the nail.

Greta's body is **8** centimeters wide.

Elvis's body is **15** centimeters wide.

Whose body is wider?

Elvis's body will be **12** centimeters wider when he is full grown. How wide will his body be when he grows up?

See page 29 for the answers.

Answers

p. 17

Benny jumped **15** centimeters higher than Callie: $25 - 10 = 15$.

p. 19

Jill has the longest ears. Peanut has the shortest ears. Jill's ears are **6** inches longer than Peanut's ears: $8 - 2 = 6$.

p. 21

Darty's toy is the longest. Gizmo's toy is the shortest. Gizmo's toy is **20** centimeters shorter than Rudy's toy: $40 - 20 = 20$.

p. 23

Leo's leash is the longest. Ollie's leash is the shortest. The difference is **10** inches: $34 - 24 = 10$.

p. 25

Sammy has the biggest bed. If it was **2** inches wider, it would be **24** inches wide: $22 + 2 = 24$.

p. 27

Elvis's body is wider. His body will be **27** centimeters wide when he is full grown: $15 + 12 = 27$.

Activities with Measurements

Measure Things Around the House

Measure the length, width, and height of your bed, your desk, your television, or anything you want!

Create a Quiz

List five different measurements in feet. Have a friend figure out how many inches each measurement comes out to. Check your friend's answers. Did your friend pass the quiz?

Write a Story

Write your own story using measurements. For example:

When Tom first brought his kitten Max home, Max was 4 inches tall and 6 inches long. The next month, Max had grown 2 inches taller and 3 inches longer. Max is now 6 inches tall and 9 inches long and still growing!

You can make it as long or as short as you want. You can even draw pictures to go with your story!

Learn More

Books

Barner, Bob. **Ants Rule: The Long and Short of It.** New York, NY: Holiday House, 2017.

Bussiere, Desiree. **What in the World Is a Centimeter? And Other Metric Measurements.** North Mankato, MN: Sandcastle, 2015.

Higgins, Nadia. **Measure It!** Minneapolis, MN: Jump, 2016.

Websites

Ducksters, Glossary and Terms: Units of Measurement
www.ducksters.com/kidsmath/units_of_measurement_glossary.php
Learn the different measurements people use.

Enchanted Learning, Measurement
www.enchantedlearning.com/math/measurement/
Learn more about different ways to measure things.

PBS Kids, Measurement Games
pbskids.org/games/measurement/
Play games to practice measuring!

Index

Published in 2018 by Enslow Publishing, LLC.
101 W. 23rd Street, Suite 240, New York, NY 10011

Copyright © 2018 by Enslow Publishing, Inc.

Library of Congress Cataloging-in-Publication Data

Names: Moldovo, Eustacia, author. | Murphy, Patricia J., 1963– author.

Title: Learning how to measure with puppies and kittens / Eustacia Moldovo and Patricia J. Murphy.

Description: New York, NY : Enslow Publishing, 2018. | Series: Math fun with puppies and kittens | Audience: K to grade 3. | Includes bibliographical references and index. Identifiers: LCCN 2017014576 | ISBN 9780766090866 (library bound) | ISBN 9780766090743 (pbk.) | ISBN 9780766090798 (6 pack)

Subjects: LCSH: Measurement—Juvenile literature. | Mathematics—Juvenile literature.

Classification: LCC QA465 .M59 2018 | DDC 530.8—dc23

LC record available at https://lccn.loc.gov/2017014576

Printed in China

To Our Readers: We have done our best to make sure all websites in this book were active and appropriate when we went to press. However, the author and the publisher have no control over and assume no liability for the material available on those websites or on any websites they may link to. Any comments or suggestions can be sent by email to customerservice@enslow.com.

Portions of this book appeared in the book *Measuring Puppies and Kittens*.

Photo credits: Cover, p. 1 Oleksandr Lytvynenko/Shutterstock.com; pp. 2, 29 (puppy, left) Liliya Kulianionak/Shutterstock.com; p. 4 Susan Schmitz/Shutterstock.com; pp. 6, 7, 9 (kitten) Anton Gvozdikov/Shutterstock.com; p. 6 (eraser) Roland Magnusson/Shutterstock.com; p. 7 (cubes) FabrikaSimf/Shutterstock.com; p. 7 (sneaker) pzAxe/Shutterstock.com; pp. 11 (puppy), 16 (puppy, right), 27 Eric Isselee/Shutterstock.com; p. 12 Tatiana Katsai/Shutterstock.com; p. 13 (chihuahua) Andrey Starostin/Shutterstock.com; p. 13 (great dane) cynoclub/Shutterstock.com; pp. 14, 15 (kitten and post) MyImages/Shutterstock.com; p. 15 (kitten, top) Lubava/Shutterstock.com; p. 16 (puppy, left) Erik Lam/Shutterstock.com; p. 16 (frisbee) Ljupco Smokovski/Shutterstock.com; p. 17 Artsilense/Shutterstock.com; pp. 18, 29 (all except far left puppy) Ermolaev Alexander/Shutterstock.com; p. 20 (kitten, left) WilleeCole Photography/Shutterstock.com; p. 20 (kitten, right) Benjamin Simeneta/Shutterstock.com; pp. 20, 21 (toy) Yellow Cat/Shutterstock.com; p. 21 (kitten, left) Linn Currie/Shutterstock.com; p. 21 (kitten, right) yevgeniy11/Shutterstock.com; p. 22 (left) Javier Brosch/Shutterstock.com; pp. 22 (right), 23 Anneka/Shutterstock.com; p. 24 (top) MarleneFord/Shutterstock.com; p. 24 (bottom) Nikolai Tsvetkov/Shutterstock.com; p. 25 (kitten) Alena OzerovaShutterstock.com; p. 25 (puppy) KalamurzingShutterstock.com; p. 26 (kitten) Happy monkey/Shutterstock.com; p. 26 (puppy) Susan Schmitz/Shutterstock.com; cover and interior pages (ruler) julichka/E+/Getty Images, (yardstick, meter stick) Siede Preis/Photodisc/Getty Images, (tape measure) Gajic DraganShutterstock.com.